Contents

Earth and Space

Our astounding cosmos
Throughout history there have been lots of changing ideas about how our solar system works. Not all of them were right!

Changing ideas
The Ancient Egyptians thought that the Sun god, Ra, travelled across the sky each day in a heavenly boat. These ideas came from their observations of the Sun as it appeared to move across the sky.

Later, the Greek philosopher, Aristotle, thought Earth was at the centre of the universe with the Sun and five planets orbiting around it. His evidence was that the Sun, Moon and stars appeared to circle Earth in the sky. Earth felt solid, so he thought it didn't move.

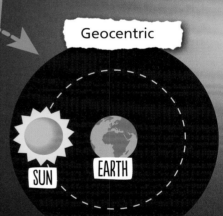

Geocentric

SUN   EARTH

The Sun at the centre
Many years later, scientists like Alhazen and Copernicus challenged the geocentric (Earth-centred) theory of the universe. They said that the Sun was at the centre of the universe and that the planets, including Earth, orbited around it. At the time, these ideas were very controversial but now we know that they are correct.

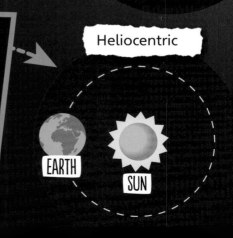

Heliocentric

EARTH   SUN

Did you know?

Galileo didn't invent the telescope but he made one so powerful that his observations could confirm Copernicus' ideas of a heliocentric (Sun-centred) universe.

Galileo and his telescope

Find out

Find out about Edwin Hubble and The Hubble Space Telescope. What is your favourite photograph taken by The Hubble Space Telescope? What does it show?

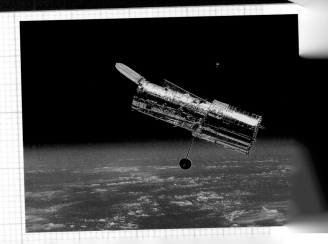

The Moon

What can you see in the Moon? Some people say they can see a man, others can see a rabbit! The dark patches we call 'seas' are actually massive lava plains created by meteor impacts.

Did you know?

American astronaut, Neil Armstrong, was the first man ever to set foot on the Moon. He did this in July 1969 together with Buzz Aldrin. Aldrin's footprint is still unchanged on the Moon's surface because there is no wind or other weather there.

the astronauts of the Apollo 11 Moon mission

The Moon's orbit

Earth orbits the Sun, and the Moon orbits Earth. Both spin as they orbit. The Moon takes about 28 days to orbit Earth. We call this period a lunar month. Because of the way the Moon orbits, we only see one side of it. As the Moon orbits Earth, the light from the Sun shines on different parts of its surface. This makes the Moon appear to change shape. We call these changes the 'phases of the Moon'.

Find out

- What did Neil Armstrong say when he stepped on the Moon's surface?
- What was the first sport played on the Moon?
- Other planets have moons too. Find out about icy Enceladus, one of Saturn's moons.

Day and night

We get day and night because Earth spins on its axis once every 24 hours. As Earth rotates, we move into and then out of the Sun's light. We call this 'day' and 'night'.

Things to do

Make a daylight diary. Find out the sunrise and sunset times for each month. Work out the day length. Plot your results on a graph. Do you notice a pattern?

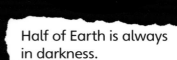

Half of Earth is always in darkness.

The International Space Station

The International Space Station is the biggest object ever to have flown in space. It orbits Earth every one and a half hours; that's 16 sunrises and sunsets in a day for them!

Find out

Find out about a day in the life of a scientist on the International Space Station. How do they eat, wash and go to the toilet?

Life Cycles

Jane Goodall

Jane Goodall is a scientist who studied chimpanzees in Africa for 45 years.

Day after day, she patiently watched how they behaved. She made careful notes every day.

From this research, she discovered that chimpanzees lived in families, had emotions and personalities, made and used tools and solved problems. No-one had ever seen this before!

Her repeated and careful observations over time led to lots of new scientific discoveries.

Find out

What else can you find out about Jane Goodall?

Jane Goodall studied chimpanzees very closely.

Life Cycles

New life

Every species or type of living thing needs to reproduce to survive. If they don't, then that species will die out entirely. Plants and animals all have a life cycle. Look at these life cycles. What do they all have in common?

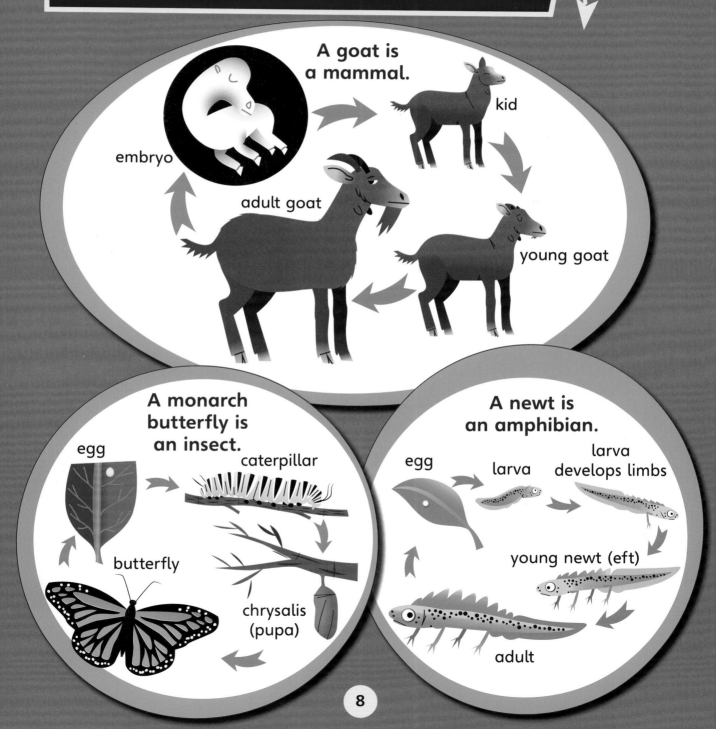

A goat is a mammal.

embryo

adult goat

kid

young goat

A monarch butterfly is an insect.

egg

caterpillar

butterfly

chrysalis (pupa)

A newt is an amphibian.

egg

larva

larva develops limbs

young newt (eft)

adult

A seagull is a bird.

egg → hatchling → young bird → adult

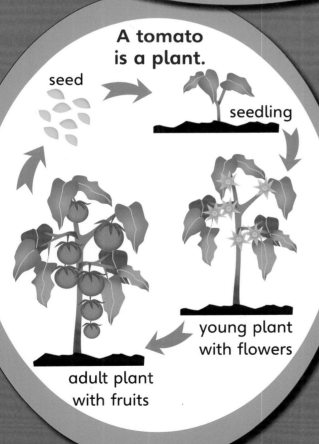

A tomato is a plant.

seed → seedling → young plant with flowers → adult plant with fruits

The circle of life

Every living thing shares a basic life cycle, with stages of birth, growth and reproduction. All living things will die eventually, but this cycle means that their offspring will go on to reproduce and continue the species.

Things to do

Some organisms have 'extra' phases or special names for different parts of their life cycles. How many can you discover? What is the most interesting life cycle you can find?

The time of your life!

Life cycles take different lengths of time. The gestation period of an animal is the time from fertilisation of the egg to the birth of the offspring.

Find out how long the gestation of various animals takes. How could you present your data? Think of two ways. Which animal has the longest gestation period of all? Why do you think that is?

The gestation time for an African elephant is 660 days!

The gestation time for a hamster is only 16 days.

Did you know?

Some birds, like parrots and flamingos, can live for over 80 years.

Some trees, like the bristlecone pine, can live for thousands of years!

Looking at variables

Bird	Robin	Blackbird	Crow	Raven
Egg				
Size (mm)	20 x 16	29 x 21	43 x 30	50 x 33
Time to hatch (days)	13	14	19	20

Is there a pattern in this data?

Which two variables can be linked?

Make up a general rule that links the size of the egg and the time it takes to hatch.

If you found an egg that was 60 mm long, how long might it take to hatch?

How long would an egg that was 35 mm long take to hatch?

Separating Mixtures

Sieving

We use sieves to separate things. A sieve has holes of a certain size. You can use sieves to separate two substances with different sized bits or particles. As long as you choose the right sieve, one substance will go through the holes and one will not.

You often find two types of sieve in the kitchen.

A colander has large holes. It can separate solid things from liquid.

A mesh sieve has small holes. It can separate solid things from liquid too.

Things to do

How many uses for a mesh sieve can you find linked to cooking?

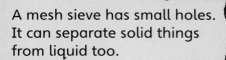
12

Sieves are not just used in the kitchen. There are some much bigger sieves that are used in industry.

Enormous sieves are used in water treatment plants. They take out large objects from the water before it is cleaned.

Farmers also use sieves to make sure they end up with just the grain when they harvest crops. The grain goes through the holes and the unwanted bits of the plants are left behind in the sieve.

Find out

Find out about other industrial uses for sieves.

Investigate it!

Identical sugar mice were given baths in different temperature baths containing the same volume of water. This graph shows how long it took each mouse to dissolve.

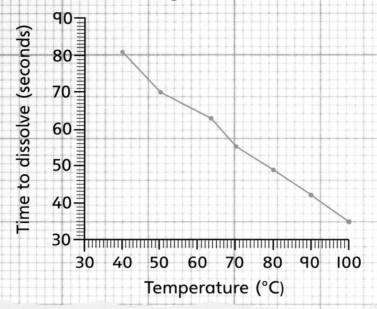

Sort these questions into two groups – those we can and can't answer using the graph.

1. In which temperature water did the mouse dissolve in the least time?
2. Do pink sugar mice dissolve as quickly as white ones?
3. How much longer did it take a mouse to dissolve at 75 °C than 90 °C?
4. Will stirring the water speed up the time taken for the mice to dissolve?
5. How quickly will a mouse dissolve at 20 °C?

Evaporation

Evaporation happens when a liquid becomes a gas. It can happen at any temperature above freezing but it will happen more if it is warmer or windier. All the particles in a liquid move but some move more than others and escape from the liquid.

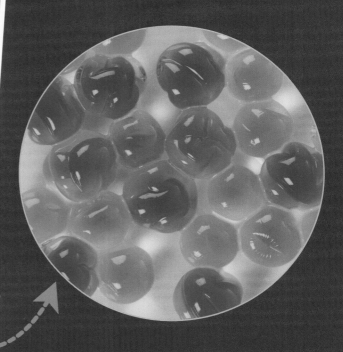

Florists often put transparent spheres that absorb water into the bottom of vases of flowers. These spheres look and feel a little bit like jellyfish and are often called slippery spheres.

Things to do

Place a slippery sphere on a plate and see how long it takes for the water to evaporate from it.

Did you know?

98% of a jellyfish's body is water. If they are washed up on a hot beach, they can evaporate and almost completely disappear!

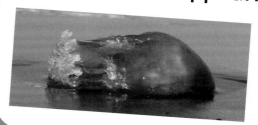

Filtration

Filtration is another form of sieving. It uses a piece of paper or fabric with tiny holes or pores as the sieve. When you pour a mixture of a liquid and a solid through the material, the liquid goes through the tiny holes but the solid is left behind.

filter paper

dirt

dirty water

funnel

beaker

clean water

Did you know?

A filter can also be used to separate solid particles from a gas. Most air conditioning units use a filter. As the air goes through the unit the filter traps any solid particles in the air but lets the clean air pass through.

Types of Change

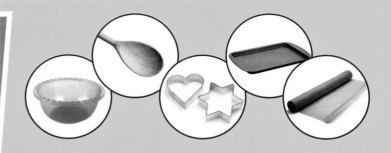

Making biscuits

You will need:
- large plastic bowl
- wooden spoon
- shaped biscuit cutters
- baking tray
- greaseproof paper

Ingredients:
- 50g soft margarine
- 50g caster sugar
- 1 small egg
- 150g plain flour
- 1 teaspoon of flavouring, e.g. vanilla extract

Instructions:
1. With adult supervision, preheat the oven to 190 °C.
2. Line the baking tray with greaseproof paper.
3. Cream the margarine and sugar together in the bowl.
4. Beat in the egg and flavouring a bit at a time.
5. Stir in the flour to make dough.
6. Roll out the dough on a lightly floured work surface to a thickness of 1 cm.
7. Cut five biscuits out of the dough.

Things to do

Put four of the biscuits into the oven and take one out every five minutes. Look at the biscuits. Describe and explain any changes that you see.

Investigate it!

A group of young scientists investigated different granulated food stuffs to find out how soluble they were.

They continuously stirred a heaped teaspoon into 100 cm³ of water at 50°C and timed how long it took the solid to completely dissolve. They repeated the investigation three times and worked out the mean average for each solid.

Here are their results:

Food	Trial 1 time to dissolve (seconds)	Trial 2 time to dissolve (seconds)	Trial 3 time to dissolve (seconds)	mean average (seconds)
salt	45	43	47	45
baking powder	24	24	21	23
cocoa powder	31	28	28	29
muscovado sugar	18	19	17	18
soft brown sugar	6	6	6	6
caster sugar	12	13	11	12

Here are photographs of all the different foods tested.

salt

baking powder

cocoa powder

muscovado sugar

soft brown sugar

caster sugar

Using the table and the photographs as evidence, decide if the conclusions the group have made are backed up by the evidence they collected.

1. All the powders are soluble in water.
2. Salt is the slowest dissolving powder.
3. Caster sugar is the quickest dissolving powder.
4. Brown powders are more soluble than white powders.
5. Sugars are more soluble than the other types of food.
6. The smaller the granules of sugar, the quicker they dissolve.
7. Instant coffee would take the same length of time to dissolve as cocoa powder because they look the same.

Melting and boiling

The melting point of a substance is when it changes from a solid to a liquid. The boiling point is when it changes from a liquid to a gas.

Metals are usually solid at room temperature because they have high melting points. Tungsten has the highest melting point of all the metals. It melts at 3,414 °C!

Tungsten is often used as the filament in light bulbs because of its high melting point.

tungsten filament

Mercury is an unusual metal. It has a very low melting point of -39 °C. So, even if you put some mercury in your freezer at home, it would still be liquid.

Mercury is a liquid at room temperature because it has a very low melting point.

Can you imagine a metal boiling? If you make it hot enough then that is just what happens. Mercury will boil at about 630 °C. To make tungsten boil you would have to raise the temperature to an amazing 5,660 °C!

Find out

Find out about the melting and boiling points of other metals.

Materials

Extreme clothing

What would you wear to survive in the extreme cold? Early humans protected themselves from cold weather by wearing animal skins.

Today, scientists have designed special clothing to help us survive in very cold places. Trapped air is a good insulator so it is important to wear layers.

The layer against the skin is called the base layer. This helps keep you dry even when you sweat.

base layer

The middle layer protects you from the cold. It is often made of a material called fleece. Fleece is light-weight and insulates you even when it is wet.

middle layer

Find out

Find out how fleece is made. What other materials are used to make the middle insulating layer?

Finally there is a wind and waterproof shell layer. This layer is made from a material that is treated with a special chemical that stops water getting in, but allows sweat to escape.

Find out

People who don't wear correct clothing when it is extremely cold can get frostbite. Find out what happens when you get frostbite.

waterproof layer

Investigate it!

May and Jay are planning an investigation to find out which type of candy laces stretch to the greatest extent before breaking. Their teacher is looking for plans which:

- describe clearly what they'll do

- list equipment they'll use

- list things they'll keep the same to make it a fair test

- plan to do each test more than once and take the average

- prepare a table to show how they'll record their results

- describe the type of graph or chart they'll be using.

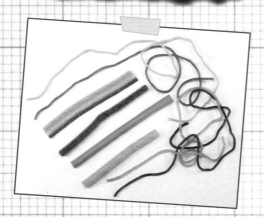

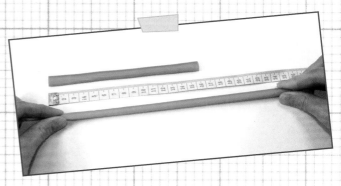

Here is Jay's plan:

- I will use three of each type of lace.

- I will pull each lace along the tape measure until it snaps.

- I will note the length just before snapping.

- I will work out the average stretch for each lace.

- Here is the table I will use:

Type of lace	Length at break point	Amount of stretch	Average stretch
strawberry		A B C	
licorice twirl		A B C	
sugar coated cola		A B C	

- I will draw a bar chart of these results.

Here is May's plan:

- For this investigation I will need different types of candy laces, a tape measure and some scissors.

- I will use laces from a new packet.

- I will cut each lace to 10 cm.

- I will trim the thicker laces so that they are all a similar thickness.

- I will pull each candy lace along the tape measure until it snaps.

- I will record the length of each lace just before it snaps.

Evaluate Jay's and May's plans. What changes would you make to their methods?

Forces

Sir Isaac Newton

Sir Isaac Newton is thought to be one of the most important scientists in history.

One day, whilst sat near a tree, he watched an apple fall to the ground. He suggested that something must be making it fall or it would have stayed attached to the branch. He named the force gravity and went on to describe how this force affects our lives on Earth.

Find out

Research the life of Sir Isaac Newton and create a mini fact file about him.

Newton meters

Newton meters are sometimes called force meters because they are used to measure forces. The unit used to measure force is called the Newton or N for short. It is named after Sir Isaac Newton.

A Newton meter has a spring with a hook attached to it. The spring stretches when a force is applied to the hook. As the spring stretches, the force is measured on the scale.

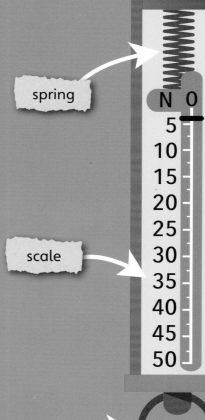

spring

scale

N 0
5
10
15
20
25
30
35
40
45
50

hook

Some Newton meters are made to measure small forces and some are made to measure larger forces. The stronger the spring inside the meter the larger the force it can measure.

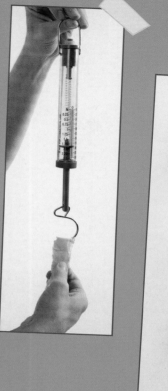

Did you know?

On Earth a force of 1N is needed to lift a 1KG weight.

Find out

Can you find out what force is needed to lift everyday objects? Try a chair or a shoe.

Simple mechanisms

Simple mechanisms make work easier.
We can use less force to do the same job.

Levers

Have you noticed how much easier it is to lift someone
when they are on a see-saw? The see-saw is a lever.
A lever is an arm that turns or pivots around a point.

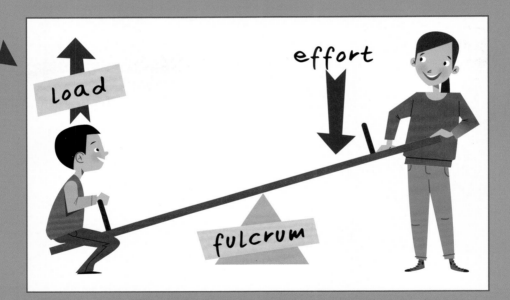

load

effort

fulcrum

everyday levers

Did you know?

Orang-utans have
learnt to use levers to
help them open fruit!

Pulleys

A pulley has a grooved wheel which spins on an axle. A rope is threaded around the wheel. Pulleys are brilliant mechanisms. They help us use less force to lift heavy objects.

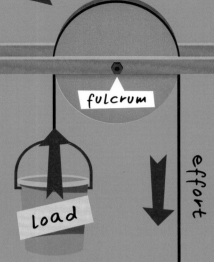

fulcrum

load

effort

everyday pulleys

Gears

Gears are toothed wheels that interlock with each other. As one wheel turns, it cause the others to turn. Using interlocking gears of different sizes can make it much easier to move things.

effort

fulcrum

load

everyday gears

Index